A Happy Trails
Christmas

★ ★ ★ ★ ★ ★ ★ ★ ★ ★ ★ ★ ★ ★ ★ ★ ★ ★

A Happy Trails
Christmas

ROY ROGERS
& DALE EVANS

Revell

a division of Baker Publishing Group
Grand Rapids, Michigan

© 2012 by the Roy Rogers-Dale Evans Rogers Children's Trust

Published by Revell
a division of Baker Publishing Group
P.O. Box 6287, Grand Rapids, MI 49516-6287
www.revellbooks.com

Previously published in two separate volumes:
Christmas Is Always by Dale Evans Rogers © 1958 by Fleming H. Revell
My Favorite Christmas Story by Roy Rogers © 1960 by Fleming H. Revell

Printed in the United States of America

ISBN 978-0-8007-2070-4

12   13   14   15   16   17   18   7   6   5   4   3   2   1

Christmas Is Always

To Reverend Harley Wright Smith
with appreciation for his remarkable
ministry to God's little ones.

My Favorite Christmas Story

To the boys and girls everywhere
whose prayers and friendship
have played such an important part in my life
this little book is humbly dedicated.

Entire Rogers family on the set of the Jonathan Winters Show, 1967

Contents

Contents

My Favorite Christmas Story by Roy Rogers with Frank S. Mead

Christmas at the Rogers'

As you all can imagine, with nine children, Christmas at our house was chaotic. We ranged in age from six months to nineteen years old. Christmas was a special time for all of us. Mom and Dad could spend some precious time at home with us kids and not on the road on personal appearances. Christmas was a time when we all somewhat behaved, because we believed if we didn't behave Santa would fly right over the Rogers' house and not stop. At least that's what Dad told us!

Like a lot of families this was also a special time to remember why we celebrate Christmas. The birth of our Savior, Jesus. Every Christmas,

Mom would sit all of us kids down in the living room so she could tell us about his wondrous birth. Mom had the most beautiful nativity scene she would set up every year. We all loved to hear her tell the age-old story. She would take out each piece of the set and explain who or what it was and what role it played in the birth of the Christ child.

What amazed me, as a six-year-old, was how many animals were in the stable at Jesus's birth. I thought, *Wow, this kid had a lot of pull to be able to have all his pets there for his birthday!*

The night before Christmas, all of us kids went to bed early. However, I got up the next morning at 4:00 a.m. Of course, no one else was up that early. I decided to see if Santa had left any cookies behind. As I passed the nativity scene, I again thought of the baby Jesus and his pets.

I thought, *We don't have one animal in this house to celebrate the baby's birth with us.* My Dad, an avid coon hunter, had several hunting dogs outside the house, and I thought that the dogs might like to celebrate Christmas with us. I decided to let a couple of the dogs in so they could see the tree and maybe have a cookie or two.

Big mistake! The dogs saw the tree and instantly knocked it to the floor. Ornaments went flying and lights went out as the hounds started looking in the tree for a coon.

Needless to say, that woke up my father from his well-deserved sleep. He stepped into the hallway and saw his prized tree on the floor, covered with dogs.

All I can say is, Dad taught me that it was more blessed to give than receive. I definitely received that morning. Oh, I enjoyed Christmas that year, but I had to do it standing up!

My hope for all of you this Christmas is that you enjoy your families. Tell each and every one of them how much you appreciate them and love them. Read the two vintage books that my parents wrote about Christmas. Please keep Christ in Christmas! Wish everyone "Merry Christmas,"

not "Happy Holidays." For this is the time for celebration of our Savior, Jesus Christ.

Merry Christmas, and may the good Lord take a likin' to ya!

Roy Rogers Jr. (Dusty)

2012

Christmas Is Always

Dale Evans Rogers

Dusty, Sandy, Marion, Linda, Cheryl, Dale, Roy, Dodie

Christmas at our house ca. 1955.

Introduction

We are too worldly wise about Christmas, too sophisticated—and shoddy. Getting and spending in order to "give," we forget what was given us at Christmas; we have lost its deeper meaning and its joy; growing older, too many of us have not grown wiser about it, but only "adult." Christmas, we say, is for children.

Occasionally, throughout this little book, Dale Evans Rogers speaks to the children. "Christmas, my child, is always . . ." or "This, my child, is a wonderful mystery." But the children to whom she speaks are aged seven to seventy; they are youngsters and grown-ups. She speaks thus to those who have had the courage to remain young in heart, to all who understand that "Except ye

. . . become as little children, ye shall not enter into the kingdom of heaven." The age of her "child" means nothing; she speaks to the hearts of all who are arrested by the mystic mystery of Christmas, who know that it is something more than a present under a tree, who would approach in childlike (not childish) faith to discover its nobler, deeper spiritual meaning. She speaks to all the yearning children of God, for whom he made Christmas.

If you insist that Christmas is just a day, perhaps you had better not read this book at all.

But if you can understand that Christmas is always and has been always, that it is not a moment in time nor a date on the calendar but "a state of heart" . . . then perhaps you had better read it . . . slowly . . . again and again. For here is Christmas as God meant it; here is the Incarnation that challenges the mind of man and warms and often breaks his heart, in such language and beauty as God might use in explaining it to his children.

Here is Christmas, my child, perhaps as you have never heard it before, certainly as you shall never forget it.

The Publishers

Christmas Is Always

Christmas, my child, is always.

It was always in the heart of God. It was born there. Only he could have thought of it.

Like God, Christmas is timeless and eternal, from everlasting to everlasting.

It is something even more than what happened that night in starlit little Bethlehem; it has been behind the stars forever.

There was Christmas in the heart of God before the world was formed. He gave Jesus to *us* the night the angels sang, yes—but the Bible tells us that Jesus shared a great glory with the Father long before the world was made. Jesus was always too!

God's Spirit has always been too; the Spirit "moved upon the face of the waters" at the time of the beginning of the world. And the Holy Spirit visited the mother of Jesus and brought forth our Lord as the Christ child, in the manger.

Christmas is always. It has been always.

But we have not always understood it.

The Magic of Christmas

When I was a little girl, the word *Christmas* was magic! It meant climbing into a railroad "sleeping car" and going from our home in Osceola, Arkansas, to my grandfather's home away down in Uvalde, Texas. It meant a happy family reunion with all my aunts and uncles and their children under the great spreading Texas roof. It meant warm weather in the middle of winter. It meant loads of "goodies" spread on the long family table, with grandfather at the head thanking God for his abundant blessings and asking that his grace be with us all. It meant a family gathering at an early bedtime around the huge fireplace in grandfather's bedroom, when we popped corn and ate fresh, luscious fruit and

said our good-night prayers. I can still see that blessed room, with the well-thumbed Bible beside my grandfather's big wicker chair. It was quite a family.

But, of course, we were still children then, and we spoke as children, and we understood as children, and it was a long time before we grew enough spiritually to understand Christmas as God meant it to be. (Too many of us, I think, never grow out of our childish concepts of Christmas!)

On Christmas Eve, down there in Texas, we always went to the church first for the lovely service, and then to the town square with its breathtaking, brilliantly lighted Christmas tree, where there were little gifts for the children. And when we woke up in the morning, there was another Christmas tree which had appeared "miraculously" as we slept; the whole family gathered around it, and again we sensed the spirit of love running through the circle. There were gifts for everyone—*but not too much*! How grateful I am for that now! The real gift was the love we had

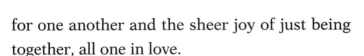

for one another and the sheer joy of just being together, all one in love.

Is this not the true Christmas? Isn't that what Jesus came to accomplish—"A new commandment I give unto you, that ye love one another"? At least, in those first childhood Christmases, we began to learn that lesson of love. The gifts were secondary; the greatest gift of all was the plain, simple gift of love.

Isn't it strange how children love the simple things? You can give a child a most expensive, intricately assembled toy, and after he has examined its color and mechanism, he will put that toy aside for an empty spool and a piece of string. Not long ago, a man I know complained of the way his boys "went through their Christmas gifts like a cyclone"—and by the end of the day had them strewn all through the house and all over the yard—and had turned to play with some empty cardboard boxes. He promised himself that "*next year they are going to get a pile of old cardboard boxes and a knife, and that's all!*"

The challenge of simplicity is a magnet to the human spirit. Much of the beauty of Christmas lies in its challenge to look further, deeper, until we find its secret in the heart of God. But we never find that unless we look beyond the presents under the tree.

Dusty, Dale, Linda, Cheryl, Roy, 1950, Encino, CA

Christmas in Our Hearts

Sometimes, when I was still a child, Christmas came for me in the summer, when we visited my father's folks in Mississippi. There I found the same warmth of family love. What a wonderful time we had in that old, rambling, two-story white house in Centerville, Mississippi. There were beautiful "summer Christmas trees" on the front lawn, adorned with velvety white magnolia blossoms. I remember the heavily loaded fig tree just outside our bedroom window; I just reached out of that window and touched it. This was Christmas too in our hearts, for there was an abundance of peace and love for God and each other.

I learned that Christmas could come on a summer's day. Christmas could come at *any* season if that sense of love were strong in the family.

Have you ever stopped to think that our Lord chose to come to earth as part of a family? He heartily approved of the family as a social and spiritual unit. When we talk about the first Christmas, do we not always see the holy family in the humble manger? It couldn't be Christmas without them there!

When we are careless about our family relationships, we are losing Christmas.

Christmas Memories

ollowing my marriage with my first sweet-heart in my teens, God blessed me with a wonderful spiritual child, my beloved first-born, Tom. It was Tom who gently led me to the feet of the Savior, many years ago, by his quiet and steady devotion to Christ in every area of his life. It was Roy's three motherless children and my feeling of spiritual inadequacy in meeting the problems of being a stepmother that made me look with longing at the serenity of Tom's face. I knew he had someone he could depend upon, and I needed that someone.

To Tom, Christmas was *every day*, for Christ was with him every day. Christ had been born *in*

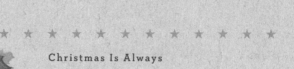

him. Every heart is, or can be, a manger in which the Lord is constantly reborn.

I have many wonderful Christmas memories, gathered as the years rolled by. Perhaps the loveliest is the one of the second and last "earth" Christmas of Robin, our little angel. I wanted so desperately to see her enjoy, understand, and really catch the spirit of Christmas, and I hoped that our carefully chosen little gifts would help and please her. You know, she looked just as though she belonged on top of a beautiful, glimmering Christmas tree. Her nurse used to call her "angel," and that Christmas day she really looked the part.

Robin was one of the greatest Christmas gifts of my life; she brought me into suffering and taught me to walk by faith with Christ through the deep waters to a new and clearer understanding of life. Through her I learned where abundant life is really to be—in the service of others through the Christ who lived, died, and rose for all of us.

I remember the indescribable feeling of happiness as I watched Robin delightedly pound the

little red piano that still sits on my windowsill . . .
and I remember hearing a song in my heart . . .

> You little blue-eyed angel,
> Heaven has sent you to me,
> You little blue-eyed angel,
> You belong on a Christmas tree.
> Hair that is gold has my precious one,
> That little smile is warm as the sun.
> You little blue-eyed angel,
> You belong on a Christmas tree.

What a blessed Christmas experience that was!
My soul grew much in understanding that day.

Dale, Dusty, Debbie, Dodie, Sandy, Roy, ca. 1960, Chatsworth, CA

A Shared Christmas

Then, the next Christmas, as we trimmed the tree for Cheryl, Linda, Dusty, and our two "newest Rogerses," Sandy and Dodie, I picked up a little Christmas-tree angel and inwardly saw little Robin's face. As I placed it on top of the tree, I suddenly knew that little Robin was very, very happy now and having a Christmas with the One who made it possible! Sandy and Dodie were ecstatic over the tree and their gifts, and we all felt warmly grateful to God for the two charming little strangers he had sent to take the place of our "angel unaware."

There was the usual Christmas turkey with my favorite Texas corn-bread dressing, marshmallow-topped sweet potatoes, "ambrosia," and

fruit cake—the Christmas dinner of my childhood. "Daddy Roy" gifted me with an electric organ on Christmas Eve, and its soothing notes proved blessed therapy to a heart remembering a little blonde head missing around the tree. It seemed the other children "outdid themselves" to help make this Christmas happy for "Mom"—because they knew I needed help.

Children are "part and parcel" of Christmas. Think how wonderful it would be if childless couples would "borrow" some orphans for Christmas!

The next time we had an addition to Christmas at the Double R Ranch was when Marion, our Scottish foster daughter, spent her first yuletide with us. I shall never forget the glow of happiness on that little face as she helped trim the tree and opened her gifts. How that child relished oranges! Oranges were so plentiful in California that we are prone to take them for granted. But I do believe that child's Yule tree was the one in our front yard, loaded with oranges!

Then came the Christmas in Chatsworth, with another new "little pixie" hanging ornaments on the tall tree in the den and piping a little sing-song Korean rendition of "Silent Night"—little Debbie! She and Dodie wanted, and got, shiny red "trikes" and little baby dolls that cried very wee wet tears.

We had nine for breakfast that Christmas morning around the huge, round oaken table, and of course, seven of them were too excited to eat! Tom and Barbara, Mindy and Candy, Grandma Smith and "Uncle Son," my brother Hillman, and Mammy and Grampy Slye came for dinner and rounded out the family, as well as five of our old "stand-by," or "on-the-loose" friends—so the place was really jumping with joy. You need something like that at Christmas; you need to share it with a *crowd*. The Bethlehem stable was crowded, you know—Christ was not born in obscurity.

As I watched little Debbie chatting happily with Dodie and busy with her toys, I felt a twinge of sadness for those countless other children in Korea,

and I wished I might have them all here too. But I thanked God that day for Dr. Bob Pierce and his World Vision, Inc., which makes Christmas really Christmas for those orphans of the storm by providing foster parents for them in America. Yes, Christmas is always . . . it goes on and on . . . in people like this. Christmas is always.

Giving

One day we all took a ride on the ski lift on Mount Summit, riding in pairs in the little suspended chairs which scaled the mountain. The higher we got, the colder and more beautiful it became. Our ascent was very slow in comparison with the descent of those who went down on their skis, just under the chairs in which we rode. What a parallel to life! To climb requires effort and persistence; to slide down, no effort at all.

At the top we jumped out of the chairs and ran into a warm "sky house" where we drank hot chocolate and warmed our toes at the big old-fashioned, round iron stove. The children were delighted with the little snow-covered "Christmas trees" which we saw on the way up—and there

were so many! Roy said, "Wouldn't it be wonderful to have one like that for Christmas, with real snow on it?" I thought of the sixteenth verse of Psalm 147: "He giveth snow like wool; he scattereth the hoarfrost like ashes."

Giving. Always, God is *giving*. Not just on one day do his gifts arrive, but always . . . constantly . . . day by day . . . hour by hour. He causes Christmas to happen with the spectacle of little snow-covered trees on mountainsides in August and July. He trims them with a color and a glory that make our hearts leap up as we behold them. He gives unstintingly and constantly of Christmas beauty to us all, if we have but eyes to see.

A Lesson in Love

So Christmas has been for me; so it has grown and developed from my childhood days. So, I think, God intended it to be: an unfolding, growing lesson in love. And as I have grown, I have come to understand that this great love must be practiced not just on December 25, but every day in God's year.

Before me is a little story written by Robert Sylvester. It reads; "The Salvation Army always has a tough time getting the right pictures to be used for each coming Christmas, and the blizzard in New York on the first day of spring this year gave them a wonderful break. The Army hurried out, found a pretty Salvation Army lassie and draped her in a red cape, broke out a standard tripod and

kettle and set it up in the snow on Fifth Avenue with the sign, 'Give a Happy Christmas.' They figured to get some good advertising and promotion pictures for next Christmas. They got them. They also got two half-dollars, four quarters, three dimes, seven nickels and three pennies—a total of $2.68—from passersby still thinking of Christmas on the first day of spring."

God's Gifts

But . . . why?

Why should there be a Christmas at all? Why did God want to do all this for us in the first place? Why? He didn't have to, you know!

You have to go back to the Bible to find the reason for it—and it isn't hard to find. This Bible was written by many men who believed in God, who prayed to God for help and understanding in their bitter, loveless world, and then listened quietly with all their minds and hearts for God to speak the truth to them. Now, God made their world and their earth with all its beauties; he was lavish with natural beauty as he finished it off, and when it was done it was perfect, and I'm sure he enjoyed looking at it. But he had something more

than beauty to lavish upon his creation; he had love to give. God wanted someone like himself, who could talk to him, love him, and obey him by enjoying this beautiful world in the way that he intended—and, of course, since God designed it all, he knew the best way. So God made man in the pattern of himself and then told the man that he could have this whole wide, beautiful world. He breathed into man the breath of life, and from that moment on man was a living soul; so the spiritual side of man too is the gift of God, the eternal Giver of every good thing.

What a Christmas present *that* was!

God was so loving and generous that he gave the man a mind like his, to think with and to decide things for himself. God gave man the superb, priceless gift of reason, for he wanted man to search for God and love him because the man wanted to, and not because he didn't know any better. Man's mind is the gift of God.

Then God saw that man, in his perfect earth, was lonely. Although man could hear God, he couldn't see him—God, his Son, and the Holy Spirit could be heard but not seen. He had formed man of the dust of the earth so man was "of the earth, earthy." Because man was lonely for a mate in his earthly paradise, God made woman, so that man could be happier and so that God could enjoy them both!

Yes, Christmas is always. It was back there in Eden, with God giving, giving, giving.

Roy, Charlie the cat, Dale • Apple Valley, CA, ca. 1995

In Bethlehem

Now the man and the woman were told by God that they could eat and enjoy the fruits of any tree in the lovely Garden of Eden except one. God knew why it would be bad for them to eat the fruit of that one tree. But the man and the woman were not as wise as God, so they disobeyed him. When they disobeyed they were not happy and God was not happy. You all know what happened after that.

The years went on, and God peopled the earth with more men and women—but they were not happy either, because the first man and woman had brought sin, or evil, into the world with their disobedience.

But God still loved them; he has never stopped loving us, no matter how evil we have become. From time to time, he would send certain men to earth who were filled with his Spirit, to try to get people straightened out and on the right path again. All he asked was that man love him as he loved man. All he wanted them to do was to love each other. But, as usual, most of the people wouldn't listen to the men God sent; they were too busy having what they called "a good time." Finally, they became so wicked that God decided to clean up the world by washing it with a gigantic flood.

God is clean and holy; he wanted his people clean and holy too. He could not bear to look down upon a world grown filthy with evil. Yet, in his infinite mercy, he gave his people one more chance: he told them through Noah, his chosen spokesman, that he would spare anyone who would turn away from wrongdoing and do what was right and worship God. I'm sure that it grieved the heart of God that no one would listen to Noah, but no one would. So "the rain descended, and the floods came" until even the mountains were covered, and only Noah and his family and the animals in the ark were alive and safe.

When it was all over, God sent a beautiful present—a glorious rainbow in the sky, with colors more beautiful than any you ever saw on any Christmas tree.

Things began all over again, and more people came to fill the earth. In time, they forgot all about the great flood, and they began to abuse the beautiful, rain-washed earth again with their wickedness. God kept sending special men to speak to them, to try to get them to turn back to him and his perfect way of life. The people treated these prophets very badly: some they ridiculed, and some they threw into prison, and some they killed. They were selfish and cruel and wanted their own way. The prophets were good and great men—but they failed.

Finally God was so concerned, and he loved the world so much, that he decided to try once again

with the dearest possession he had: his own Son. He would send his own Son to earth; perhaps they would listen to him!

He knew that his Son would have to be born like a human being, and live and look like a human being, in order to reach human beings. God wanted his Son to be accepted on earth; he also wanted to show the people of earth what the Father, our God, was like.

God looked the world over and chose a young and pure maiden named Mary to be the mother of his Son. Now, God could have put his Son Jesus Christ on earth in any way he wanted, but wasn't it an indication of his love that he chose to honor a human being in allowing her to be the mother of his child? What a present that was for Mary!

God decided to make the arrival of his Son startlingly different from what the world expected. So, the night of his Son's birth, he sent a heavenly host of angels to announced the birth to humble shepherds on a hillside in Judea. What a present for *them*!

The world expected the Christ to arrive in a scene of dazzling splendor, like a king from heaven. But no—God planned it otherwise. He made the scene of the nativity radiant with the simplicity of a lowly manger, with Joseph, the husband of Mary, and the shepherds, and the beasts of burden in the stalls round about. Instead of princely robes of velvet and satin, our Lord was wrapped in swaddling clothes and lay in a bed of straw.

You can still see the spot where he was born, in a little rock-lined room cut into the hillside of Bethlehem. Thousands make their pilgrimage there every year to stand in awestruck silence for a moment—for the greatest moment of their lives. No one ever laughs there; many weep. To no other being ever to live upon our earth is such homage paid after 1900 years. As we go in to see the manger-spot, we pass through a little door cut so low that we must bow to get through it. No man, woman, or child approaches this holy spot without a bow.

No matter which day in the week you go there, it is Christmas. Christmas is always, in Bethlehem.

One of many photos of Dale and Roy taken in the Apple Valley snow for inclusion in the annual Christmas letter.

The First Christmas Gifts

A s the heavens are higher than the earth, so are my ways higher than your ways" saith the Lord. Our Savior's coming had been predicted by the prophets centuries before, and even the kings of the Orient, far from Bethlehem, were eagerly watching for a sign of his arrival. They were so vigilant in their waiting that they recognized immediately the bright new star in the East and started down the long, long road that led to Bethlehem, to see this long-awaited Messiah. Imagine their surprise when they found him in a stable!

But perhaps it made no difference, for in the pictures we have of them standing at the manger, we see no surprise on their faces. They stand there in their rich, royal robes, or they kneel there

offering their finest gifts of treasure. One offers gold; hereafter, gold is good enough only to be thrown before the feet of Jesus Christ! Another offered frankincense—a sweet-smelling incense often burned at the altars of the temple. Frankincense, as well as gold, is useless now; it was not holy ritual but holy living that this Christ demanded. One offered myrrh; this babe would die young, on a cross, and Mary, happy now, would need myrrh for the embalming.

These were the first Christmas gifts from human hands to God. Study them well; they have deep meaning.

Even then, God was saying to the wise and the mighty: "Except ye . . . become as little children, ye shall not enter into the kingdom of heaven." What did God mean by giving us this babe, by this lowly birth? Was he not giving him as a Christmas present to the poor and as a rebuke to those who put their trust in riches?

As he grew to manhood, Christmas was everywhere that Jesus went. He gave lovingly to friend

and foe alike. He gave of his divine nature to heal the sick, to raise the dead. He changed water into wine at a wedding feast, fed thousands on a hillside with a few loaves and fishes, made the blind to see, forgave guilty, miserable men and women and transformed them into new, victorious people by his matchless words.

Imagine the joy of Jairus, a ruler of the synagogue, brokenhearted at the death of his twelve-year-old daughter, when Jesus took the dead child by the hand and lifted her up into life again! What a Christmas for that family!

Think of what must have gone through the hearts of Mary and Martha when their brother Lazarus walked out of that tomb after four days! That was really Christmas, for, you see, Christmas is giving and Jesus really gave of his divine strength to revive those loved ones from the sleep of death.

He has been doing it ever since: millions have been lifted out of the sleep of unhappy, purposeless lives into abundant life by the gift of faith in

this Christ. On whatever day they accepted this gift from him, that day is Christmas to them forever.

How much Christmas he gave! Remember the time when the mothers all crowded around him with their little ones, and how he put his strong, tender hands on each of them in blessing and how his followers complained of his taking so much time for the little ones when there were so many weighty matters to be discussed, so many other more important things to be done? What did he answer? "Suffer little children . . . to come unto me: for of such is the kingdom of heaven." He was saying that Christmas is for the young in heart, and that only those with the simplicity of a child's heart can appreciate Christmas and his gifts. Those who become so wise in their own eyes that they think they do not need Christ—these have lost the wonder, the true magic, the glory of Christmas.

Receiving

Yes, my child, Christmas is giving in the name of Christ. But—Christmas is also *receiving*! Is that hard to understand? It shouldn't be. What would you think of the Christmas "spirit" of a friend who wasn't even grateful enough to thank you for a present? If he has the Christmas spirit at all, he will receive it with joy and gratitude and thanks because of the love which prompted the gift. The Bible says that God so loved this world that he gave his only son, and that "as many as receive him, to them gave he power to become the sons of God." As many as *received* him! When we understand that, we understand that receiving is even more important than giving at Christmas!

Let me illustrate what I mean. Suppose a child had an overabundance of beautiful toys, and he

saw a poor, ragged little fellow with no toys at all. He would feel sorry for the luckless youngster and offer him one of the best toys he had as a present. But—he says he doesn't want it! He still looks unhappy when he says it. So the benevolent one picks out another and offers that, and *that* one is rejected. He tries several times, and finally offers him his favorite toy, the one he loves best, the one he really wanted to keep forever. The other looks at it for a moment, shrugs, and turns away. This would be too bad, wouldn't it? This could have been a real Christmas for the boy, but he wouldn't receive the gift.

Can you imagine how God feels when he offers us his only son, and we reject him, even crucify him on a cross? You see, my child, to really receive Christmas you must receive Christ first; the rejoicing comes later.

What does it mean to receive Christ? It means to understand that he came into the world to save sinners, and that we are all sinners by nature. We need to be saved from our sinful natures, or, as the

Bible says, to be "born again." Or, if you will, "made over." When we receive Christ and take him into our lives and let him make those lives over, then we receive the Supreme Gift, for he comes into our hearts through his Holy Spirit, and we experience the gift that is Christmas, the joy of union with God, and peace on earth and good will toward men.

Christmas is not just a date on our calendar; it is a state of heart.

The folks who have the best time on December 25 are those who have received him and give in remembrance of him. Suppose we set up a different Christmas tree this year! Suppose we set one up in our hearts. Suppose the tree is Jesus Christ, the True Evergreen, the Life Everlasting. Suppose we adorn this tree with the gifts he brings to those who accept him—love, forgiveness, patience, hope, charity, peace, mercy, understanding, humility. Suppose we turn on the lights of this tree very brightly and *keep* them on! If we do this, our "traditional" tree will take on a new and richer meaning.

Dale and Roy, Apple Valley, CA

Like a New Tree

Speaking of the Christmas tree—trees, you know, have been historically recognized as symbols of everlasting life. That is, no tree ever dies; it leaves new life behind it in seed and acorn. Job says that "there is hope of a tree, if it be cut down, that it will sprout again," and we are told in the first Psalm that one who loves the Lord "shall be like a tree planted by the rivers of water." It is all symbolic of the rebirth of Christ in the human heart. Every time a repentant and seeking heart says, "I believe" the king and Lord of all is born anew in the humble dwelling of the heart.

The Christ child in us must be allowed to grow, and we allow him to grow like an everlasting tree as we, his branches, bear fruit fit for his kingdom.

This, my child, is a wonderful mystery, but it happens. I have seen it and experienced it.

The Bible says that the human heart is by nature deceitful and desperately wicked. But Jesus wants his home there so that his Spirit can change that heart. You know, when once I opened my heart to Christ in sincere faith, I was just like a little child seeing her first "Christmas tree." All of a sudden everything around me looked new and beautiful and shining. I was like a new tree "planted by the rivers of water." It was the crowning Christmas of my life.

Traditions

The Christmas tree is traditional; so is Santa Claus. We've always had him around at Christmas; he's really a tradition!

But just what does Santa Claus have to do with Christmas, anyway? And how did *he* get into the picture?

Well, my child, the figure of Santa Claus is actually a symbol of the truly Christian spirit of giving, in spite of what some people say about him. He represents a man named Nicholas who, according to tradition, lived many, many years ago in Asia Minor. Nicholas's father was a very rich merchant who for years had no children. He and his wife prayed and promised God that if he would send them a child, they would train him to love and serve God. God answered their prayer

and sent the boy, whom they named Nicholas. He was carefully and lovingly nurtured and well educated in the Christian faith.

His parents died, however, when he was quite young and left him a great deal of money. The Spirit of the Lord prompted Nicholas to give away all he had, with the exception of three small bags of gold, which at that time would have kept him nicely for the rest of his life.

One day he overheard the weeping of a neighbor's daughter, and he heard the father say to the girl that he was too poor to give her a dowry for her marriage. (In those days a girl could not marry unless she had a dowry, or a gift of money, to bring to her husband; if she could not do this, her father had to sell her as a slave.) There were three daughters in this family, and they all wept when they were told they could not have a dowry. The girl who was at the marriageable age wept loudest of all; she was the one Nicholas heard, and he couldn't bear it. He had all three bags of his gold at this time; he crept behind a bush under the window of the neighbor's home and tossed one of his three bags of gold through the window. He did not want them to know who did it, for he remembered the words of Jesus: "When thou doest alms, let not thy left hand know what thy right hand doeth: That thine alms may be in secret: and thy Father which seeth in secret himself shall reward thee openly."

So the daughter was happily married. Then came the next daughter's turn. The father was still poor, and again Nicholas heard the weeping. Again he secretly provided the dowry by tossing his second bag of gold through the window.

By this time, the father was determined to know who their "angel of charity" was—so when it came time for the third daughter to marry, he stationed a watchman outside the house to catch his wonderful benefactor. Sure enough! As Nicholas tossed in his last bag of gold, the man grabbed him and took him in the house, where a very grateful father thanked him for insuring the future of three tearful but very grateful girls.

Of course, this became known in the town, which embarrassed Nicholas, for he was a modest young man. Since he loved to serve God and his fellow man, he decided to become a priest. When he had finished his studies, he returned to his home town of Myra in western Greece. Myra was having quite a time of it right then, trying to elect a new bishop to preside in their cathedral to take the place of the old bishop who had just died. The clergy just couldn't agree on the man to fill the vacancy so they decided to wait until the next out-of-town priest walked into their cathedral, and they would make him the bishop.

While all this was going on inside the cathedral, Nicholas came along the main street of the town. Just outside the cathedral he found a crowd of little children and he stopped to talk with them (and, I like to think, even *play* a little with them!). Then he stepped into the cathedral—to be welcomed by the shouts of the clergy, who then and there proclaimed him the new Bishop of Myra.

Nicholas became known as "the patron of the children" for his untiring efforts to help them and teach them. Each year on his birthday, which was December 6, Nicholas would collect presents and distribute them among the children. This idea of presents for the children spread all over Europe, and it was always done in memory of St. Nicholas, who was such an outstanding example of the Spirit of Jesus.

The word "Santa Claus" is the Dutch name for St. Nicholas, and we adopted "Santa Claus" when the early Dutch settlers came to New Amsterdam, or New York, as it was called later. The English called him "St. Nicholas" and sometimes "old Kris Kringle," but whatever they called him, they always associated him with the giving of gifts at Christmas. In the town of Myra, after Nicholas died, the practice of giving gifts continued on December 6 for a long, long time before it was finally transferred to December 25.

The red robe of Santa Claus has a religious significance too; it represents the red "cope" (or cape)

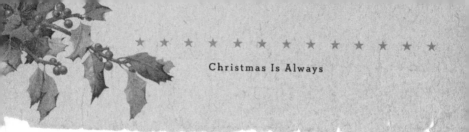

which the priests of the church wore at Christmas. The fur-trimmed hat and boots were adopted by the cold countries of the north; travel there would be very cold and very difficult for Santa unless he had a sled and some fast reindeer—so he got the deer and the big sled, and he became a jolly round old man distributing untold happiness to children everywhere. He was never meant to overshadow the celebration of the birthday of our Lord Jesus Christ, but only to supplement it, for it was the Spirit of our Lord that gave us "St. Nicholas."

Christmas photo, Chatsworth, CA

The Meaning of Christmas

Someone is asking, "If Christmas is always, as you say, then why do we set aside December 25—just one day in the year—to celebrate it?" Well, there's a lot of tradition in that too. We might answer that question by asking, "Why do we stop work one day a week—on Sunday—instead of on Thursday or Friday?" The answer is that God gives us that one day in the week to rest, to think about what happened last week and what will happen next week, to renew our strength through prayer and meditation so that we can face whatever comes. We *can* rest on other days too, of course, but having a special day set aside for this seems to impress upon us our need for

refreshment and for the remembrance that we need to stop and "take stock of ourselves."

The same thing can be said of December 25: it is the yearly reminder that our Lord loved us enough to become one of us, to sacrifice himself for us to that we might understand once and for all *that God is, and always was, and always will be; that God is Love, and that love will win, even on a cross.*

Love is the greatest power there is, and love is the meaning of Christmas. This is why we need a day set aside for remembering the "earth birth" of our Lord, who was Love clothed in human flesh. Christmas is the day set aside for us to ask ourselves whether we honestly love God and man. We need this day of spiritual inventory to clean out the old worthless stock of indifference and to restock our hearts and minds with the Spirit of the Christ, to receive him and give ourselves.

Christmas, my child, is love in action. When you love someone, you *give* to them, as God gives to us. The greatest gift he ever gave was the person of his son, sent to us in human form so that we might know what God the Father is really like! Every time we love, every time we give, it's Christmas!

The Greatest Gift

So let's put *our* love into action this Christmas. How?

Wouldn't it be nice to visit Christ this Christmas by visiting those imprisoned by sin or sickness?

Wouldn't it be more Christlike for us to visit someone in need of food or clothes instead of exchanging a lot of gifts and gadgets which have little use?

Somewhere on the plains of Kansas there is a humble doctor who spreads the Christmas spirit in a chain reaction. As Christmas day comes closer and closer, the doctor writes every patient who owes him anything, canceling the bill as a sort of Christmas present! But . . . there is one little

condition: the patient must contribute a similar amount to a worthy charity. The doctor writes the patient: "Send us their receipt and we will close your account." It is a four-way gift: from the doctor to the patient to the charity—and on to the unknown man or woman who benefits by it all! Why not try *that* this Christmas? Why not try a little actual forgiving of our debtors instead of just mumbling it over in the Lord's Prayer?

Instead of worrying about what we should or should not pay for a gift for a friend, how about a donation for an orphanage in his name? You could send him a card saying that he has shared in some Christian Christmas giving with you.

How about offering Christ your talent this Christmas instead of some of your money? He wants the best you have to give, not the cheapest! Do you know the story of "Why the Chimes Rang"? It deals with a set of church chimes that rang only when someone offered a gift that came from the heart at Christmas. The rich gave their gold—no, gave *some* of their gold—but the chimes were silent. The not-so-rich gave "what they thought they could afford"—and the chimes did not ring. Finally there came a lame boy who had no money at all; he laid his crutches on the altar—and the chimes rang! I've always had an idea that the boy walked out of the church with a new strength, leaving the crutches behind.

Sacrificial giving to God always rings the bell.

How about giving up a grudge or a grievance or an imagined hurt this Christmas to get a little peace in your heart? "Peace on earth, good will toward men!" That heavenly announcement is printed on many of our Christmas cards. Do you know, my child, that many years before the Savior was born, a prophet named Isaiah foretold the birth of Jesus and said that he would be known as the Prince of Peace? Later, this Prince of Peace told us that peacemakers are blessed—or happy. What he meant was that unless you have peace you can never be happy. Another time, he said that if we have anything against our brother, we should be reconciled (or make peace) with

him before we offer a gift to God in his place of worship.

In Czechoslovakia, I am told, the people celebrate Christmas by visiting their friends and foes and forgiving any misunderstandings which might have arisen during the year. Christmas to them means the ending of old quarrels and the beginning of the new year among new friends. God must love that! He never gives us his peace until we have drowned every hate and grudge and bitterness in the great sea of his love and mercy. Only when we are at peace with others do we have Christmas in our hearts.

Or, you can gather up some of the things you don't use anymore, get them to one of those organizations that mend and restore them and send them out to folks who are in need. Remember the joy each item brought you: wish the same joy to the one who receives it from you, and you will find out how blessed it is to give with such a wish. For wishes, like thoughts, are things; this way, you will be sending two things—a wish and a useful gift.

While we are at it, how about a real sacrifice this Christmas? Like choosing one of your most prized possessions and sending it out to someone to express your love? God gave us not "something he could afford"—he gave his most precious possession in heaven, his own son!

We need to see his son beyond the gilt and gadgets of Christmas, need to see him in the manger, in the streets, on the cross. Christmas is like the walking of Jesus, like the moving of the Spirit from the days when time began to our own times, like the redemptive purpose of God working out its way in our lives through the one born at Bethlehem.

Yes, my child, Christmas is always, for Jesus said, "Lo, I am with you alway," and Christmas is Jesus!

Dale and Charlie the cat, 2001

My Favorite Christmas Story

Roy Rogers

with
Frank S. Mead

Christmas Is Real to Roy

In the following pages you will read what Roy Rogers feels about Christmas.

In 1945, one day during the filming of one of his Western musicals, Roy and I were discussing our sentiments about Christmas. He said, "I can't understand anyone not appreciating a gift, no matter what the size. When I was a kid, we didn't have enough money to buy all the things kids get nowadays for Christmas. But I loved my one toy—a brand spanking new, shiny pocket-knife! You know, a kid in the country without a pocketknife is a lost cause! I whittled my own toys all year with that Christmas knife. One Christmas day it slipped out of my pocket and I cried so hard

and so long that Pop had to go buy me another one next day!"

To this day, Roy's face lights up like a Christmas tree when he receives a gift. What a smile! But the greatest smile I ever saw on his face was the night he received the Gift Supreme—eternal life through putting his faith in the Lord Jesus Christ as his Savior. This indeed was Christmas in the heart of Roy Rogers, for instead of a pocketknife, he received the shining sword of spiritual truth with which to fashion a new wonderful life! I know—for I was there and witnessed it.

Roy does not like to write, but he is quick to give reason for the hope that is in him. He gave this to our good friend, the esteemed editor of Fleming H. Revell, Dr. Frank S. Mead, and we are grateful to him for rounding up Roy's Christmas thoughts.

Dale Evans Rogers

I'm Fed Up with Christmas

That sounds a little stupid, doesn't it, coming from a fellow who goes to church as often as he can and who prays regularly and who thinks the Christ born at Christmas is the greatest gift God ever gave to anybody—including me? Maybe I'd better explain what I mean, so you won't think I'm a turncoat or a crank.

What I mean is that I'm fed up with what a lot of us are *doing* with Christmas. Out here in the West we have a weed we call loco; it grows wild in the range grass, and it drives the cattle loco, or crazy, when they eat it. I think we have all gone a little loco about Christmas—like those crazy cowboys who shoot up the town on payday in the

movies. We've almost shot Christmas to pieces, and that's wrong, in my book.

You can see it in a lot of the stories that are written every Christmas by good folks who mean well enough and who can write better than I can, but who miss the target by a mile when they sit down to tell us what Christmas is all about and how we ought to celebrate it. Some of those stories are good—like Dickens's *Christmas Carol*—but too many of them are a waste of time to read. I've just read one of them, about how some fellows spent Christmas Eve in a night club, and how they chipped in to buy a kid a lot of toys. They probably spent ten times more on highballs that night than they did on the toys, but they went home to sleep it off (on Christmas Day!), real happy that they'd "kept the Christmas spirit." There was another story about a youngster who grew up to be a famous prize fighter; he got a set of boxing gloves for Christmas, and he spent the best part of the holiest day in the year slugging his pals dizzy and getting slugged dizzy himself.

That's *Christmas*? You can read a whole carload of stories like that, and you won't find the Bethlehem baby in one of them.

Maybe I'm getting a little soft in the heart (I hope so!), and maybe I'm just a sentimental cowpoke, but I don't get it. To me, leaving the baby out of *any* Christmas story is like leaving the salt out of your food. Any story that does that is as useless as the pony express or the stagecoach.

For me, there's only one Christmas story. It sticks up like Pike's Peak. It has made all sorts of people happy for nearly twenty centuries, and it'll be told twenty centuries from now. Every time I hear it or read it I feel like singing, or going off somewhere to just think about it and let it run warm through my heart.

It's my favorite Christmas story. A tax-collector named Matthew and a doctor named Luke tell it in the Bible, and it goes like this . . .

Born in Bethlehem

"Jesus was born in Bethlehem of Judea in the days of Herod the king."

That was about two thousand years ago, and it happened 'way off in a little town in one of the smallest countries in the world. I'll bet there wasn't one in a thousand in the old Roman Empire who could tell you where Judea was, or one in ten thousand who could tell you how to get to Bethlehem. Funny, isn't it, that people all over the world this year will be thinking and talking about Bethlehem and the baby born there? Or maybe it isn't so funny at that; God planned it that way.

We'll all be singing about Jesus, but nobody will be singing about Herod, the "king of Judea." There was a mean polecat, that Herod. He was one of those ornery characters who will do anything to get what he wants. He wanted to be a king, and he really went after it with his guns out of both holsters. He murdered his favorite wife (he had ten wives, and I guess that was one thing that was the matter with him), her brother,

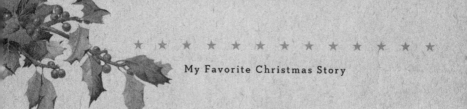

and her grandfather, and some of his own children; he bribed anybody low enough to be bribed among the politicians, and he killed anybody he couldn't buy, to get that throne. It's a good thing he didn't have a six-shooter or a machine gun; there wouldn't have been anybody left. He was mean and deadly, and so were the Romans who were running the world and Judea right then. The Roman emperor probably didn't like the little murderous upstart, but he knew a determined man when he saw one, so he said to this little Hitler, "All right—you can be king of Judea." (Judea was only about fifty-five miles long and fifty-five wide, smaller than the state of Delaware, which looks like a pretty small "kingdom" to me.) "All right, you can be king of Judea. You can rule for us. Just make the people behave and be a good boy yourself, and do what we tell you to do, or else." That's how Herod got his little sawed-off kingdom. He got to be "king of the Jews," and every Jew from Dan to Beersheba hated him like we hate a rattlesnake. (Herod wasn't a Jew, even though he was born in Palestine; he was an Edomite, and no Jew ever liked *any* Edomite.) He built a big beautiful temple for the Jews in Jerusalem—and clobbered them with new taxes to pay for it. They didn't like that. This was the temple Jesus saw in Jerusalem. He didn't think much of it either.

That's the way things were, "when Jesus was born in Bethlehem of Judea in the days of Herod the king." There was fear and terror and bitterness and blood all over the place. And poverty. There wasn't enough freedom to put in a ten-gallon hat; it was all blood and sweat and toil and tears. And taxes.

God got tired of Herod along about AD 4 and took him out of the way. That's a habit God has; he seems to let the big bloody tyrants and trigger-men go just so far, and then—out! He took Herod, but just before he died the old rascal put on a real spectacular. He heard that a new "king" had been born in Bethlehem (five miles from Jerusalem), and he figured that while this "king" might be no king at all but just something made up in the

minds of a lot of superstitious people, he couldn't afford to take any chances. No king likes a rival king. So he ordered his soldiers to go out and kill every baby in Bethlehem. It's hard to believe that even as vicious an hombre as Herod could think up anything like that, but the Bible says he did.

Herod lost out, at that. The baby was taken out of Bethlehem just in time, and the soldiers never found him. And a little while later Herod died, and the baby grew up to be a king with a kingdom and a power that Herod never dreamed of: he became king of the human heart.

This I believe, because he's king in my heart, and because I believe in Christmas.

Old Herod was gone. But there were still taxes.

There Went Out a Decree

"It came to pass, in those days,
that there went out a decree
from Caesar Augustus, that all
the world should be taxed."

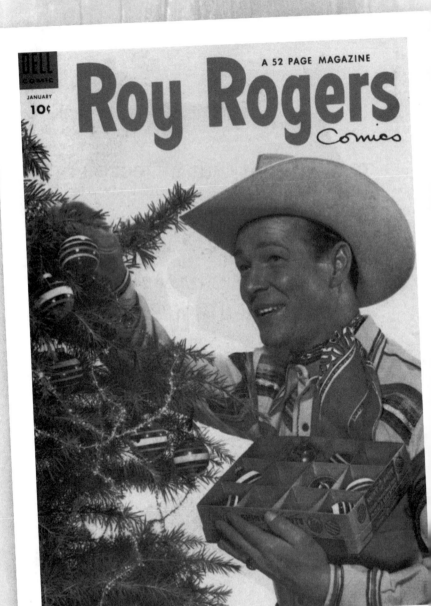

We pay taxes in the United States, and we grumble when we pay, and we say it isn't fair. We should have been around when Caesar Augustus was foreman of the ranch! If you were a Jew in Judea in his time, you paid and paid and paid. First of all, you paid Jewish taxes: you paid for the support of the temple—which meant paying to keep the priests, who really had it good; every male Jew over twelve years of age kicked in to keep those priests living in luxury, on the fat of the land; he paid a half-shekel poll tax, or "temple tribute." There was also a tithe on crops, cattle, wheat, figs, olives on the tree and grapes on the vine, barley, and honey. Whenever a special day or event came around, there was a tax to help you celebrate it: when a firstborn son came along, or a male animal was born, you paid a five-shekel thank offering whether you were thankful or not; if you sinned you paid a tax whether you were sorry about sinning or not; you gave meat

"offerings" and "trespass" offerings and there was always a "special drive" for some special purpose being put on by the priests and temple elders.

When you had paid up your Jewish taxes, Caesar Augustus and his Romans went to work on your pocketbook. They taxed you for the fine "Roman" roads they built across your land; if you crossed a bridge in your travels, you paid a Roman bridge tax; if you went to the theater, they got you again; if you went into the temple Herod had built to the emperor's glory in Samaria, you paid. You couldn't get a drink of water or a mouthful of food without paying off the Romans; you even paid a salt tax to flavor your food. You paid property tax, village tax, city tax. To help Caesar pay his retired soldiers a pension, there was an additional "purchase" tax. If the Romans improved your town, you got the bill and you were supposed to be grateful for the improvements.

If you bought or sold anything inside Judea or beyond Judea, you paid a tax; you even paid a tax when you went up to the temple to pray. You paid, or they took your house and your land; they could draft you into the army or sell you into slavery if you didn't pay cash on the line. The tax collector could put a false value on your possessions, and you paid; or they could loan you the money for the tax, and charge you 25 percent interest! If you died, there were "death duties." It was nice, for Caesar Augustus. He got rich, and poor Judea got poorer; how much he took out of there, we'll never know.

Augustus may have wanted to build himself a new palace in Rome when he decided that "all the world should be taxed." He didn't spare anybody; the whole world was to pay him. And in order to know just how many he could collect from, and how much he could load on each man and woman, he took a census. "And all went to be taxed, every one into his own city." That meant that every man and woman in Palestine had to go and register and sign the tax-roll in the city or town his family came from.

Up in Nazareth lived Joseph and Mary; they packed up, and started down the long road to Bethlehem, the town of Joseph's family. Joseph didn't exactly like the idea of that trip, for Mary was about to have a baby and Bethlehem is sixty miles from Nazareth, as the crow flies. By the way of the long twisting road, it was nearly ninety, and Joseph didn't own a car and there were no buses or railroads, so they *walked*. Joseph walked, anyway; the artists who have painted pictures of it show Mary riding on a little donkey, and I guess they are right, for no woman about to give birth to a baby could have taken a hike like that. Joseph was a carpenter, with good muscles, but Mary . . . even on a donkey . . . ninety miles!

She was so sick and exhausted by the time they got to Bethlehem that she couldn't have gone another mile. I wonder what she was thinking when they came into that little town after dark; I wonder if she was remembering what her cousin Elizabeth had said to her, some time before: "Blessed art thou among women, and blessed is the fruit of thy womb." How blessed was she now—so tired she could scream, and without a roof over her head or a place to lie down and sleep? What was blessed about all that?

Yet in her heart she knew how blessed she was, for God had chosen her, out of all the women in the world, to give the world this baby. This wasn't Joseph's baby at all; this was the Son of God waiting to be born in Bethlehem. I think the blessedness came back to her when she thought of that, and while she was a little afraid, as any mother is afraid when any baby is born, she knew everything was going to be all right. God had chosen her, and God would see that everything was all right.

You see, it wasn't any accident that they were in Bethlehem that night; even Caesar Augustus had little to do with it. Long ago, as a child, Mary had read in the old Jewish Scriptures, in the book of Micah the prophet, a promise that this child of hers was going to be born in Bethlehem: "But thou, Bethlehem . . . though thou be little among

the thousands of Judah, yet out of thee shall he come forth unto me that is to be ruler in Israel." Mary knew this. She knew her baby was the Promised One, the one promised by the prophets and the Book and God. She knew she was the blessed "handmaid of the Lord" through whom the Son would come.

That's what fascinates me about Christmas. It isn't just a day to pass around presents to everybody, or one day in the year when you're nice to everybody whether you love 'em or loathe 'em; *this is the day God Almighty chose to give us his only begotten son, through Mary of Nazareth.* How can we miss that?

Most of the folks in Bethlehem missed it when poor frantic Joseph knocked on the door of a little inn and asked for a room.

No Room in the Inn

"There was no room for them in the inn."

here is something about that knock of Joseph's that hurts. If Joseph and Mary were to ride into your town tonight, you'd have a heart; you'd take them into your home or phone for an ambulance and get them to a hospital. Most of us would do that, because that's the way we are after two thousand years of Jesus Christ. But people weren't like that in old Bethlehem; they were suspicious of strangers, especially strangers who arrived in the middle of the night. They didn't put "Welcome" on their doormats in those days. They wouldn't have opened the door for a stranger from Galilee, because the people up there were rough and tough, always fighting the Romans or fighting among themselves. Galileans weren't popular anywhere but in Galilee!

The courtyard of the inn was jammed with donkeys and camels and swearing, weary men. The inn was crowded; there wasn't even standing room. Joseph must have known there wouldn't be

any room for him and his Mary, but he knocked anyway. What else could he do?

Knock, knock, knock. A baby is about to be born. The most important baby ever to be born on this earth. Let us in, let him in, out of the cold and the night. Knock, knock, knock.

The sleepy innkeeper came rubbing his eyes, and opened the door. He didn't waste any words; he just told them there wasn't any room. They'd have to go somewhere else.

"No room." They are the most heart-rending words in the Bible. No room. Would you have said that? *Don't* you say it, every day? Don't you say it to Christ when he asks you for your heart: "Go away and let me sleep. I've got no time for you, no room in my heart. . . . I don't know you"? We're all innkeepers, with room for everybody and everything but him. Not many of us really let him in. I heard once about an old Scottish minister who used to go around knocking on the doors of his town and asking whoever answered the knock, "Does Jesus Christ live here?" People stared at him and told jokes about him. They thought he was crazy. But was he? Did those jokers wisecrack to cover up a guilty conscience?

But you know, sometimes I feel sorry for that innkeeper, just as I feel sorry for anyone who turns a cold shoulder on Jesus Christ. He just didn't know what was happening, and what he was missing. He just said "no room"—as cold as the ice in Alaska. I think he'd have taken them in if he'd known. Maybe we've been a little rough on him, criticizing him as we do. To me he was like a fellow wandering in a desert, stumbling along in the night past a spring of cold water he couldn't see and didn't even know was there.

No room. That's what he said. Then—I figure it this way—his wife came up behind him and took one look at Mary on her donkey, and told them to go out to the stable. The inn was a rambling old building, with a sort of patio in the center, and around this patio they often carved little caves out of the soft limestone rock for the pack animals of the travelers who stopped at the inn, or

for their own sheep and oxen and donkeys when the weather got real cold. It just could have been that the innkeeper's wife thought of one of those stables—a woman *would*—and that she fixed up a bed of clean straw, and covered Mary and sat with her awhile. A woman would do that, for women think with their hearts more than men. The innkeeper was all business; his wife could have been a mother.

I wonder how long we'd keep Christmas if it were up to the men.

Born in a Stable

"She brought forth her firstborn son, and wrapped him in swaddling clothes, and laid him in a manger."

So the baby was born in the cold, unfriendly night, in a cave cut in the side of a hill, in a bed of straw, in a stable. In Bethlehem, when you ask to see the place where Christ was born, you are taken to a little rock-bound room. There is a big stone church built above it now, with great high beautiful pillars and altars with gold and silver and precious stones, but people who go there now never pay much attention to that. They hurry through the church and take little candles in their hands and go down a flight of narrow twisting stone stairs worn smooth by the feet of saints and sinners and scholars and common folks, into the little rock cave underneath the floor of the church. They stand there hushed, some of them with big tears running down their cheeks, and they look down at the big golden star set in the floor to mark the place where the manger was, where he was born. Princes and paupers come, high and low, good and bad, just to stand for a

few minutes where the innkeeper tried to turn Joseph and Mary and the baby away. They come into the place through a door that's only four feet high, so low that they have to bow to get through it. No matter who or what they are, they bow as they approach the manger.

You stand there, and all the world stands still around you, and you hear nothing and see nothing but the baby in the feeding-box where the oxen came to eat, and if you've got a heart, it breaks.

That's Christmas, to me; standing at the manger.

It was a stable, yes, a mean place for a baby to be born, a mean place even for animals. It wasn't nearly as fine a stable as Trigger has. It wasn't the light, shining place the artists have painted; it was a dark, damp hole in the ground. Here he was born. You don't like it? You think the Son of God should have been born in a palace, or at least in a place where there wasn't any dirt or darkness? But that wouldn't have been right, because God was sending his Son into a world that was a filthy stable, a world dark with pain and hatred and dirty with sin. It was right for him to be born here, for he had come to make men clean and to bring a light into the world that would drive away the darkness in men's minds. I'm no theologian, and I haven't had an education in theology, and I know this explanation of why he came may not please all the theologians, but that's the way it looks to me. I can't put it in fancy language, but I can say that he brought light and peace and something new and clean and fine into my life, and that's all the theology I need.

Some of the highbrows in Jerusalem got mad at him once because he sat down with a lot of low-brow sinners and outcasts that the "best people" just didn't associate with. They criticized him for that; he turned on them and told them he had come to help people like this, and not "the best people," who were so proud and self-righteous they thought they didn't need any help. Some of his best friends were sinners. He came to get them out of the stable.

Dale and her horse, Buttermilk, Christmas parade, 1950s

Shepherds Abiding in the Fields

"There were in the same country shepherds abiding in the field, keeping watch over their flock by night."

★ ★ ★ ★ ★ ★ ★ ★ ★ ★ ★ ★ ★ ★

After Mary and Joseph, the animals in the stable were the first to see baby Jesus in his swaddling clothes. Maybe there was a young calf there, and maybe that reminded the Jews in the inn that his people had once worshiped a golden calf. Or an ox: there were some people who worshiped oxen. Or a sheep, marked for sacrifice that week in the temple at Jerusalem. But now that the baby had come, the sacrifice of animals was on the way out. Men would not worship or sacrifice beasts any more—they would worship the Christ who lay in the straw. The breath and the warm bodies of the animals warmed him in the little room. If they could have talked, what would they have said to him? What would the lambs have said to the Lamb of God who would be sacrificed on a cross?

The animals—then the shepherds from the hills. The shepherds were the first men to come. The

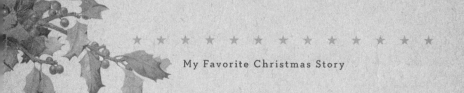

people in the courtyard may have looked in at him, and smiled, and gone away never knowing what they had seen, but the shepherds *came*, and they came because they knew, and they came to worship. Out on their hillsides, watching their sheep, they had heard a great strange music. If *you* will go out this Christmas Eve and stand still and just look up at the stars and listen, you can hear it too—the music that comes from behind the stars, from another world. You can hear it, if you'll listen.

The shepherds heard the angels sing: "Glory to God in the highest, and on earth peace, good will." Peace? For the shepherds, who got kicked around by everybody? Good will? Who had anything good to say about a shepherd? You were really out of luck if you had to watch sheep for a living; that was about as far down as you could go. But my Bible says the shepherds heard it first, and that they came first to worship the little king who would make them the equals of anyone in the world. They had waited a long, long time for

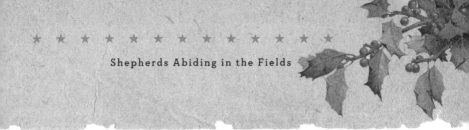

this night—ever since Abraham was a shepherd in Ur, ever since David was a shepherd in Bethlehem, they had waited. Now they came running into Bethlehem, *believing what the angels had told them*. They came first because they were the first to understand that this was the Good Shepherd.

They were poor, so they couldn't have brought any Christmas presents—oh, maybe a little milk, or wool, or a baby lamb. But their gifts weren't important. *They brought themselves*. It was all the baby would have wanted from them. Did you ever stop to think at Christmas that the only gift Jesus wants from you is you?

Christmas is giving time—time for giving ourselves.

We don't think enough about those shepherds. We talk about how they came to Bethlehem; how about looking a how they *left* Bethlehem? They left it "glorifying and praising God"—and man, that's important. I'll bet they sang all the way home. Anyone who meets Jesus Christ goes away

singing. It's a little like going to church; you can't go there without feeling better.

Something happened to the shepherds. They didn't go home and sit around the rest of their lives dreaming about what happened that night. They told everybody about it, and "all who heard about it wondered." It figures. They had to tell everybody. I never knew a happy man who was a quiet man, who could keep his mouth shut about whatever it is that is making him happy.

Christmas is telling time—wondering time. Wonder enough about it, and you'll know, and you'll tell about it.

My mother and father told me about these shepherds when I was a kid, and I never could get them out of my mind. These shepherds never went to school, never wrote any books, probably couldn't read or write. But they were the first Christian preachers; and I've got a sneaking suspicion that the folks who listened to them didn't care very much that they couldn't read or write, or that they were shepherds. The people knew they were listening to eyewitnesses. Some of the best preachers I've ever listened to never saw the inside of a college, but they had something inside them that was good, and they threw it right at me, and it stuck. I think the shepherds were like that.

Once I heard about an old hermit down in Egypt, who lived four hundred years after the shepherds were dead and gone. This old fellow lived in a cave, where he worshiped God day and night, at a time when the scholars and the bishops and the theologians in the city were getting themselves—and everybody else—in one grand and glorious snarl arguing about Jesus Christ. Some of them said Jesus was just a man, and some said he was just God and not man at all, and some said he was the Son of God, and . . . It all got pretty confusing. After a while they brought the old man into town. They asked him if he thought Jesus was the Christ, the Messiah. They figured he'd know, if anybody did; he lived so close to God for so long that the people were

calling him a saint—Saint Anthony. He looked at them in amazement, and he said, "I have seen him!" He had seen the Christ, and he knew. So had the shepherds.

Christmas is seeing time. If you can't see him then, you may never see him.

usty, Linda, Dale, Cheryl, Roy, Trigger Jr., Hollywood Christmas parade, 1950s

Wise Men from the East

"Behold, there came wise
men from the east."

The wise men came to Bethlehem too. Do you suppose the shepherds met them on the road? If they did, what did they have to say to each other?

These wise men came from the East—that could mean from Persia—and if you know what I mean, they were big league, or something special. The kings in the East were pretty powerful; the kings told the people what to do—but the wise men told the kings. They knew just about everything there was to know about what was going on in the world—*and* in heaven! They had all the answers; they read secrets in the stars and they came all the way from Persia guided by a strange star they had never seen before, as a ship is steered by the stars. They came down the same old road the Queen of Sheba had come down, a thousand years before, to visit Solomon, the wisest man in the world, to ask him questions and give him gifts of gold and rare perfumes.

They turned up in Jerusalem first; I'd guess they got off the road, or that one of King Herod's patrols picked them up and brought them in as suspicious characters, for questioning. And I'd guess old Herod was scared half out of his wits too when he saw them. He'd heard the gossip about the baby "king" born in Bethlehem, and he didn't like it; if this Bethlehem baby was all people said he was, there could be trouble. All these people who hated the sight of Herod could start a revolution around the king in Bethlehem. There must be *something* to it; these wise men hadn't come all the way from Persia for nothing.

Herod was clever, though; give him credit for that. "All right," he said to the wise men. "All right. Go to Bethlehem and see what's going on down there, and then come back and report to me, so I can go and worship him." There was murder in his eye when he said it.

So they went out and looked up in the sky for the star, and—"when they saw the star, they rejoiced with exceeding great joy." They found him

there in the stable, and they got down on their knees and worshiped him.

Then they unpacked their bags and laid out on the floor of the stable the gifts they had brought all the way from Persia. They were gifts you'd never buy in a five-and-ten-cent store, for these men were rich as well as wise. They brought gold— and laid it at the feet of Jesus Christ, at the feet of one who was to be poor until he died, who was born in a borrowed manger, who was to eat borrowed food at the tables of his friends, who was to die on a borrowed cross and be buried in a borrowed garden, who was to say to a man with much gold, "Sell all thou hast and give it to the poor." At his feet the wisest men in the world threw their gold, as if they were saying, "You're right. Your way is best." It was something new. Up to then, you measured a man by his gold, by the size of his strongbox. You were somebody if you were rich, and nobody if you weren't. This baby—did the wise men know it?—gave us a new yardstick for measuring the worth of a man; you

Roy and Trigger Jr., Hollywood Christmas parade, 1950s

were somebody, he said, if you were a servant. Gold had a brand-new use: it was good only to help others, to help the poor.

They gave him frankincense. Let's call it incense, for that's what it was—a sweet-smelling offering that was burned in the incense pots of the temple. The Jews burned incense in their great rituals in the temple at Jerusalem, and the wise men, all their lives, had seen it burned in their pagan temples far from Jerusalem—burned as wistful, wishful offerings of faith and hope before the unmoving idols of the pagan world. It rose up into the faces of these clay-faced gods. Of course the gods couldn't help, but the worshipers were sincere enough; their burning frankincense had to do with the things of the spirit, and that was good.

But it was better, now, to bring incense to a *living* God. And when they dropped that incense at the feet of this living God in Christ, they were offering *their* lives as incense too. They were adding living to ritual, if you know what I mean.

God demands that of all of us: he wants our lives burned out for him. If we can't give him our lives, we might as well save our incense.

It's something like this. You know my horse Trigger? He's pretty smart. We do quite a few tricks together at rodeos and county fairs. Trigger can dance, step around to music, and he can take a bow like a real ham actor. It looks so easy—but it takes days and weeks of practice on the ranch in San Fernando Valley to get those tricks smooth and right. We go through a sort of ritual at the rodeos, and the folks like it. (Maybe ritual isn't the right word, but you'll know what I mean.) But a lot of the folks will never know how much practice it takes before we get out there. It takes a lot of practice to make a Christian—*a lot of good living*.

So here in the stable the wise men threw their precious frankincense at the feet of Jesus, as if they were saying, "From now on we'll burn out our lives in your service."

And myrrh. They gave him myrrh. Myrrh was even more important than frankincense; it was an expensive perfume (the Chanel No. 5 of the court ladies), and the priests used to put it in the oil they used to anoint other priests and kings and the sick. It was a gum from the myrrh tree that relieved pain; the Roman soldiers gave Jesus wine mixed with myrrh while he hung on the cross. And Nicodemus brought myrrh for the embalming of his body when Jesus died. But they couldn't have been thinking of all that when they brought it to the baby in the stable; it was just a rare costly gift fit for a king. I wonder, though, if they might have been thinking a little about healing—about the healing of broken hearts and lives, and the "healing of nations" that had come to earth with this baby. Wealth, worship, healing . . . it could be.

Three wise men from the East, bearing gifts. We don't even know their names; they are supposed to be named Caspar, Melchior, and Balthazar, but the Bible doesn't name them. It doesn't even say there were three of them. There might have been more, or less. It doesn't make much difference. It wasn't how many of them there were but what they did that counts.

They brought gifts—expensive gifts. Is that where we got the idea that we all have to break the bank to buy expensive gifts at Christmas—that we have to go broke to prove we've got the Christmas spirit? I get sick all over just standing in the stores at Christmas time, watching people throw their money around like loco cowboys on payday. They put on mob scenes that would go good in the movies, fighting each other to buy a lot of over-priced junk (you can get it at half price the day after Christmas!) that most of their friends don't want, with money they haven't got, or shouldn't be spending if they have got it—for what? We beat our brains out trying to think of something to give someone who doesn't need anything. I saw a sign in one department store that told me this was a department filled with expensive odds and ends "for the man who has everything." Well, if

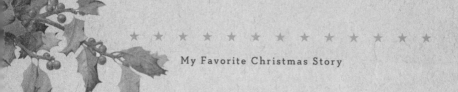

he has everything, why give him more? Maybe he'd appreciate it more if you'd come around to see him when he's sick, or give him a hand when he's in trouble.

There used to be a society called SPUG—"The Society for the Prevention of Useless Giving." Whatever became of that? It was a good idea.

Why do we do it? Why do we commercialize Christmas like this? Do we have to throw money away to prove we aren't "cheap" about Christmas? To me, we cheapen ourselves when we celebrate the King's birthday with a one-day spending spree, and then forget him all the rest of the year. If that's the Christmas spirit, I don't want it.

Sure, the wise men brought gifts—*for Jesus Christ*. They gave *him* their gold; they gave *him* their frankincense and myrrh. And they took something away. They didn't just drop their presents under the tree and say "Merry Christmas" and then go out and forget it until next Christmas. *They turned their backs on an old, wrong way of life and walked off with God*. They brought their gifts to God, not to any man; they saw God in the manger, and the sight of him made them different men.

Christmas shouldn't be spending time; it should be changing time.

Going Home a Different Way

*"They departed into their
own country another way."*

hat's what Matthew says they did after they had left their gifts: they went back by a different road. Oh, yes, they were "warned of God in a dream that they should not return to Herod," but to me that's only half of it. I think they'd have gone home that way even without that dream; old Herod would have killed them, and they knew it. The important thing is that the road back was *different*. Everything was changed. Every hut and stable gleamed with light. Every woman was a Mary. Every crude, cursing man was loved of God, with a new friend back in Bethlehem. Every shepherd seemed a new kind of man, a man with ears tuned to hear the angels sing. It was a different road, a different world. God was in it now as he had never been in it before.

The shepherds first, then the wise men: first the lowly, then the great. I've always been glad those wise men came, even if they did get there a little late. They were running true to form, coming

late; the fellows with lots of brains *always* come late. They have to fight their way through a lot of brain-problems that never bother the rest of us—but they come. The really intelligent man comes to the manger and gets down on his knees. The greatest astronomer always finds his star and stands silent as he looks at it.

I'm told there's an island in the Caribbean Sea where a lot of Yale and Harvard professors spend their vacations every summer, and that on the island there is a blacksmith who teaches a Sunday school class for grown-ups. The professors come every Sunday to hear him; it's the best part of their vacations. They just sit and listen to him. He's got something they never found in books—and they want it.

The *really* wise always come.

Going to Bethlehem

*"Let us go now even
unto Bethlehem."*

I s'pose I'll be in California this Christmas. I'd like to be in Bethlehem. Wouldn't you? Well—let's go! Let's have a Bethlehem Christmas this year, wherever we are. We don't have to travel. All we have to do is to turn our hearts into a manger and let him be born there. Can I ask you something here, without making you mad? *If he isn't born in your heart, what difference does it make to you whether he was born in Bethlehem or not?*

I heard another good story the other day. Seems there was a little girl looking at the nativity scene they'd set up in her church for Christmas. She looked a long time at the face of the little wax doll they'd laid there in the straw to represent the baby, and then she said, "He's a lot more alive than that." Smart girl! She said it for me. She saw what I wish all of us could see in this great Christmas story: that Bethlehem is *now*, that he is here just as much as he was in the stable of

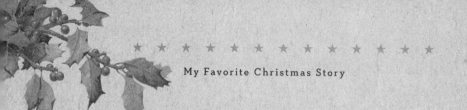
the inn that night, waiting for us to come, to give ourselves.

Let's all go even unto Bethlehem.

May the good Lord of Christmas take a liking to you, and a Bethlehem Christmas to you all.

Roy, Trigger Jr., Santa, Linda, Cheryl, Dusty, Dale

Roy and Dale, 1960s

Christmas is a time for *miracles*.

Cozy up with this romantic and heartwarming tale of unexpected love.

Revell
a division of Baker Publishing Group
www.RevellBooks.com

Available Wherever Books Are Sold
Also Available in Ebook Format

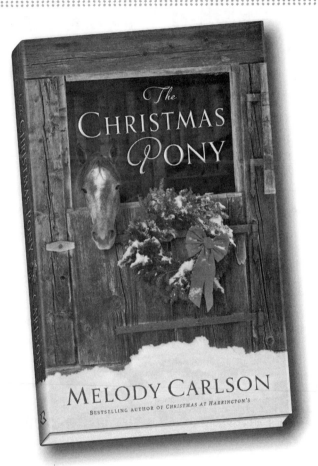